NINE WORLDS
← IN →
NINE NIGHTS

A Journey Through Imaginary Lands

TO THE READER

In 2018, Walker Books were approached by Emily Furness, niece of the late Professor Dawn Gable, the prize-winning theoretical physicist. She presented us with a collection of writings, drawings, paintings and souvenirs found amongst her deceased aunt's possessions which she thought we should see. This astonishing material describes the Professor's travels through nine fantastical worlds in a phantom machine, guided by a beastly apparition and a book with a mind of its own.

Incredible as this account may seem, we were compelled to share the story. We now present the collection to you, alongside the worlds the Professor visited, taken from the pages of her "Magic Book".

Prepare to open your mind to all possibilities...

WALKER ! STUDIO
AN IMPRINT OF WALKER BOOKS

Prof. Gable, final term, Cambridge

PROFESSOR DAWN D. GABLE

PhD, MRI, MInstP

WHAT FOLLOWS IS A COMPLETE AND ACCURATE ACCOUNT OF

MY TRAVELS WITH HYLLVAR
ᒧᐊ ᐳᒉᐊᐃᑕᐯ ᐁᒌᐳᑊ ᐳᐸᒡᐳᒉᑊ

HOW IT BEGAN
ᑭᒉᐁ ᒉᐳ ᑌᐃᑕᓕ⊡

It all started on the 6th of January – my birthday. I hated birthdays
and was at my desk working as usual when, to my great irritation,
I was interrupted by the doorbell.

On the doorstep were two children. The girl was holding a package
wrapped in gold paper. "Yes? What do you want?" I snapped. "It's ME,
Aunt Dawn. Your niece, Emily," the girl spluttered. "And this is Tom,
remember?" I was shocked. These were my brother's children whom
I didn't recognise as I hadn't seen him or them for years. "Where's
your father?" I asked. "In the car," said the girl, "but we know
it's your birthday and we've brought you a present." She pushed
the package into my hands. "It's magic," said the boy. "That's why
you're to have it. Dad says you need it!" And they fled.

Magic indeed! Dad says I need it! I fumed. What could he mean and
what was he thinking sending his children to disturb me? And why
now, like this, out of the blue?

I tossed the unwanted gift aside and went back to work, but around
midnight I was drawn to it as if by some unseen force. Tearing off
the wrapping I found an old, highly illustrated book and its title
– LOST IN THE IMAGINATION – was warning enough. It was filled with
images and descriptions of worlds invented by dreamers, fantasists
and folklorists – worlds my brother and I had loved when we were
young but which he knew full well I had no time for now.

Infuriated, I slammed the book shut and threw it across the room.
It landed in the fire but, astonishingly, did not catch alight.
While flames hissed and spat around it, it lay untouched, its cover
glowing like a stained-glass window.

Lost
IN THE
Imagination

• TEMET NOSCE PRESS •

What occurred next is hard to put into words but as the point of any journal is to record what happened exactly as it happened, I have no choice. A creature, like a figment of dreams, rose from the smoke and stepped towards me holding the book out in scaly paws. I wanted to scream or run but I couldn't move or make a sound. The thing came closer, stinking of ancient forests, and introduced himself in a low steamy bark which, against all reason, I was able to understand. "Hyllvar, descendant of Nidhogg, the ancient Norse dragon. At your service. And I know who you are. You are your own worst enemy. Imprisoned in a cell of guilt and denial."

At this outrage my voice returned. "And what are you?" I fumed. "Some smoke and mirrors trick conjured up by my ridiculous brother? Well, I'm not taken in. I deal in hard facts and here is one — you are not real." The thing shrugged, lumbered to the door and steamed, "Real or not, we offer you a chance, your brother and I. One chance, your only chance. Pass it up and you'll be beyond anyone's help, for I alone can show you what no other can or will — nine worlds in nine nights to fire your imagination and save you from your desolate, fact-bound life."

"How dare you threaten me or assume I need help," I raged. "Now disappear or I will end you by forcing myself awake!" Undeterred, the beast barked, "Protest as you like, but you are stuck, and you know it. You are grounded, like a bird with a broken wing, going nowhere and going alone. So live or die, come with me. Or die inside anyway."

It was this that got to me. It cut me to the bone for it was true. I was alone and stuck, dying inside, without new ideas or inspiration, each day feeling as if I were pushing treacle uphill.

My resistance finally dissolved and, insane as it was, I now rose to a challenge laid down by an apparition and followed the thing into the driveway, where the madness of the night would literally get wings.

A Machine from a Far-Off Future

At first there was nothing to see except a thin veil of falling snow before the flakes parted to reveal a machine as unthinkable as the creature leading me to it. As we approached the lights flashed, a bubble-dome opened, the legs withdrew and it came to rest at ground level, compacting into some kind of craft that might orbit the moon in a science-fiction fantasy. Although I did not yet know it, this was only one of the transformations this unearthly contraption would be capable of.

HYLLVAR'S FLYING MACHINE

In its first form, drawn as accurately as I was able to observe and remember.

1. Two sets of modular wings transformable to meet different travel systems

2. Antennae for sending and receiving data

3. Energy-dense external navigation lights

4. Bubble-dome command module with voice-activated dashboard, steering system and crew/passenger space

5. Segmented body housing power modules and heat shields

6. Solar panels to derive electricity from sunlight

7. Retractable, segmented legs that serve as launch thrusters and enable rapid movement across any surface

Hyllvar

Hyllvar left me alone to stare in awe and disbelief. By the time he barked an order to board, I was over the shock and ready to see just how far these theatrics could go. I climbed in beside the beast and his aura of dank forest and, with barely a sound, we were airborne. Time ceased to exist and then, in a few moments or several years, I could not tell, we were landing.

The First World

Deeply shaken, I now experienced the first of the Machine's transformations as it seamlessly turned into a land vehicle and scuttled like a giant mechanised scarab beetle over the steep, rocky landscape. Arriving amongst ruins in the valley below, I saw the remains of an ancient temple and cried out in disbelief, for this was certainly the temple of the lost city of Kôr — one of the worlds I'd glimpsed in the Book before I threw it at the fire. I yelled at Hyllvar that it could not be but the beast shrugged dismissively. Then, fading before my eyes, as apparitions will, he said, "Be curious. Curiosity will take you further than you can dream."

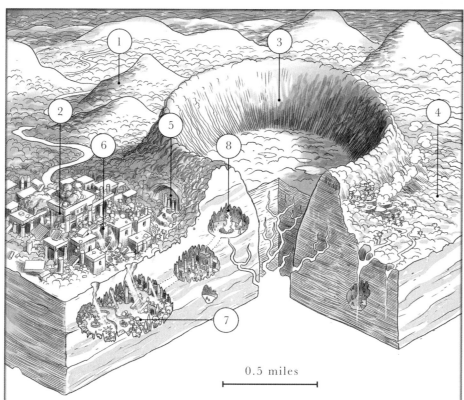

0.5 miles

– RUINS OF KÔR –
CROSS-SECTION

1. Mountainous rocky terrain above the valley

2. Ruins of the ancient city

3. Caldera of the volcano, extinct around 11,700 years ago

4. Dense forest on slopes of the volcano

5. Abandoned temple

6. Entrance to the old catacombs

7. Gardens of Princess Ayesha's palace in the catacombs

8. Fire of Eternal Youth and Beauty

THE LOST CITY OF KÔR

Kôr, built around a vast dormant volcano in the East African Rift Valley, pre-dated the Egyptian pyramids and was once the capital of a great civilisation eventually wiped out by a plague. Now, a dangerous, all-powerful princess named Ayesha who claims to be immortal, able to read minds, heal wounds and cure illness, has her palace in the catacombs. From here she rules over the Amahaggers, a fearsome tribe of mountain forest dwellers, who call her She-Who-Must-Be-Obeyed.

Hyllvar may have disappeared but I was not
stepping out of a phantom machine into a fictional
world — until two small men with painted faces
started hammering on the scuttler's dome.
Terrified, I opened it and let them march me
across sand-whipped ruins into an underground
palace. Here they left me, awe-struck, in a
sumptuous throne room. Carried away by the
grandeur, I opened a jewelled gate. It led to
a cavern cut into rock where a giant Pillar
of Fire was burning. As I approached, a veiled
woman stepped from the shadows and pushed me so
close I smelt my hair singe. "It is by bathing
in this fire that I have gained my eternal youth
and beauty," she whispered. "Is that what you
want? Is that why you're here?" "No!" I cried.
"Then go," she ordered, "before you get more than
your fingers burnt." Wrenching myself from her
grasp, I ran, any way I could, out of the palace.
Thankfully, the painted men found me wandering
in a nearby forest filled with amazing plants and
creatures, and guided me back to the Machine.

– THE THRONE ROOM –

*Monumental engraved columns support cave ceiling. The pure gold
throne sits beneath a canopy of elaborately carved blackwood.*

– PRINCESS AYESHA AND THE PILLAR OF FIRE –

*The Fire of Eternal Youth and Beauty. Ancient Egyptian
glyphs inscribed in the rock walls.*

– FLORA OF THE SCRUBLANDS –

KNIPHOFIA.

Commonly known as Red Hot Poker

RED-VEINED DROP-WING DRAGONFLY:

Common across Africa

PYRGOMORPH GRASSHOPPER:

Bright colours indicate toxicity to insect-eating birds

HARTLAUB'S TURACO:

Vivid blue, green and red plumage and a distinctive red eye ring

TACAZZE SUNBIRD:

Largest of the sunbirds, mainly found in open highland and bamboo forest

AFRO-MONTANE GIANT LOBELIA:

Stores water in its rosettes

COLOBUS MONKEY:

Hunted for its soft, silky fur, the only monkey not to have thumbs

MALACHITE SUNBIRD:

Glistening green feathers on the male in breeding season only. Insect and nectar-feeder.

AFRICAN LEOPARD:

Grows to over 6 feet in length with tail as long as 3 feet. Nocturnal carnivore who hunts at dawn and dusk.

DENDROSENECIO OR GIANT GROUNDSEL:

Found at altitude, can grow up to 20 feet tall

I climbed in, dazed. Was this actually happening? Had I nearly been pushed into a burning Pillar of Fire by Princess Ayesha? Dimly aware of Hyllvar beside me in the Machine, but with no sense of how long it took, I was home and hurrying across the driveway to the sanity of my house. I sat down at my desk thinking I'd shake off the night as a wild aberration and get back to work. Instead I found myself furiously sketching some of what I'd seen that night in the way one is compelled to write down an important dream before it recedes and is lost forever. Deciding I would properly research everything at some later stage, I eventually pulled myself away and went to bed.

The second World

I slept fitfully through the rest of the day, trying to reason as I tossed and turned. Dragons do not step out of fires speaking English, I told myself. Kôr does not exist. Clearly I was the victim of a hoax, arranged by my brother who lived his life in the theatre surrounded by illusion and trickery. If I kept my head, normality would resume. But when I got downstairs the Book lay open on "Mecanopolis — City of Machines". Lights from the phantom craft flashed through the window. I grabbed the fire poker and ran out to try to damage it but Hyllvar was waiting to disarm me. "Do you turn down a chance to observe the development of conscious machines? Not even you can be that dull," he sneered. I could not bear to be so patronised and, with gritted teeth, climbed aboard and let myself be flown into a spine-chilling world of intelligent machines.

1. **Charging stations**
   Source of pod power

2. **Art gallery**
   Where masterpieces are automatic

3. **Automated Bowlerama**
   The balls bowl themselves

4. **Spare parts kitchen**
   With three-dimensional printers

MECANOPOLIS – CITY OF MACHINES

In Mecanopolis everything is done by machines for machines. There is no organic life, not a plant, person, bird or animal. There is a Museum of Humans where the machines exhibit, for their own study or entertainment, products and reminders of the human race that lived in their world before them. Travel is via lightways and suspended highways and the city is serviced and kept spotless by an army of self-driven robot-mechanics, cleaners and polishers. Printers capable of producing three-dimensional objects provide spare parts for repairs.

5. **Stadium**

For sporting events

6. **Auditorium**

Automated orchestra performances

7. **Museum of Humans**

Remains and artefacts

8. **Cleaner-bot service**

station and terminal

We soared into the city over awe-inspiring mountains of metal, glass and chrome. As our Machine fitted right in, we moved easily amongst the other formidable machines, ground and air robots, pods and automata that soared, swooped, floated and sped with alarming purpose and velocity. Each place we visited was more startling than the last, especially the inhumane Museum of Humans. The whole city foretold of some future robot uprising when artificial intelligence would take control of our planet and organic life would be a relic of the past. None of the robotic inhabitants paid us any attention until we turned off one of the suspended lightways and found ourselves in what I can only describe as a pod-wash.

surveillance bot

Recording bot

Pod-wash cleaner

Torch bot

— NANO-BOTS —

— THE AUDITORIUM —

Concert hall where the instruments of the orchestra play themselves, performing continuously without beginning or end.

— ART GALLERY —   Where exhibitions of masterpieces created by robot brushes and robot sculpting tools are displayed.

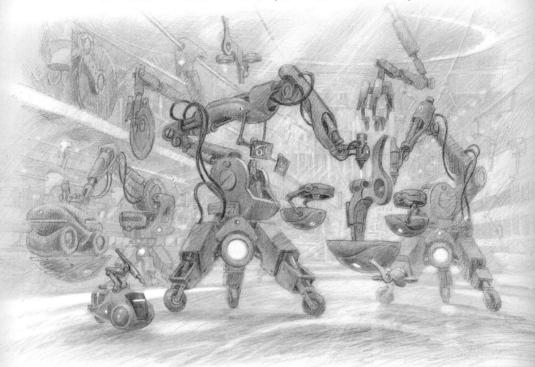

Where machines print out parts for other machines, and robot mechanics carry out repairs.

- ROVING MICRO REPAIR BOT -

About the size of a cotton reel.

- MUSEUM OF HUMANS -

Showing specimens of the extinct human species and its artefacts. Examples of the type of food we eat are on show and another display makes fun of our forms of transport.

The outside of our Machine was instantly swarming with cleaner bots. At first none took any notice of the human and the "dragon" inside but then I saw a gleam of intention on one. "They're coming in!" I cried, quite terrified at the prospect. "I'll end up in the Museum! Look!" The front hatch of the Machine shifted, letting in a thin sliver of acidic neon light. "Quick! Lock the doors!" I yelled. "Lock them!" Hyllvar, as cool as ever, calmly touched the instrument panel. We reversed at supersonic speed onto a lightway and were streaking through steel-grey skies into the dawn breaking over my house. Safely inside I saw the Book closed on the table. To my despair, it opened itself on Camelot, court of King Arthur. Whatever all this was - real or imagined - I had to call time on it or conclude I might be going mad.

The Third World

I slept deeply and when I awoke night had fallen. There was no Machine, no Hyllvar and the Book was closed. With relief, I sat down to work but again found myself drawing – this time the machines and scenes in Mecanopolis – until I got so cold I couldn't hold the pencil and ran out to get wood for the fire. Groping blindly in the dark, I stumbled and fell and must have blacked out because when I came round I was lying on a bed of damp leaves under a canopy of oaks. Through the rising mist I made out distant mountains, forests and a towering castle. This was certainly Camelot, court of King Arthur and his knights, in legend and in lore.

Arthur, Merlin & Guinevere

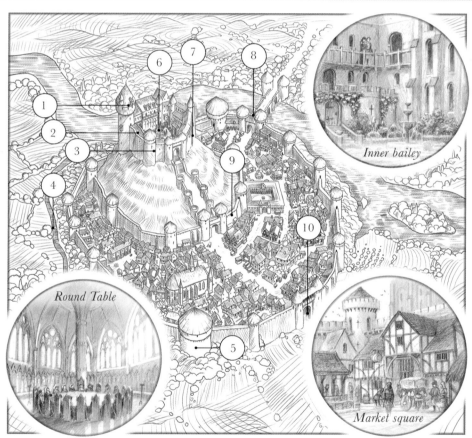

Inner bailey

Round Table

Market square

– THE CASTLE –

1. **Keep** – *fortified tower*

2. **Ramparts** – *defensive wall topped with a walkway*

3. **Arrow loops** – *slits in towers and walls for shooting arrows*

4. **Moat** – *deep water-filled ditch; preliminary line of defence*

5. **Barbican** – *outer fortifications*

6. **Bailey** – *enclosed courtyard*

7. **Buttresses** – *wall reinforcements*

8. **Drawbridge** – *bridge that can be raised to prevent entry*

9. **Battlements** – *parapet provides cover for patrolling soldiers*

10. **Portcullis** – *heavy grilled gate lowered on chains*

CAMELOT – COURT OF KING ARTHUR

Camelot Castle is where King Arthur and his wife Queen Guinevere hold court. From here, with his knights and the guidance of a wise wizard named Merlin, Arthur goes out to defeat invaders, tyrants, troublesome beasts and malevolent magic in order to establish a unified, peaceful kingdom. Arthur became king at the age of fifteen when he alone, amongst nobles from far and wide, was able to pull out a heavy sword from a great slab of stone. As king, Arthur was presented with a sword named Excalibur by a lady who rose from a lake. It has an unbreakable blade and, as long as he keeps its scabbard buckled at his side, he will never lose blood in any battle or skirmish.

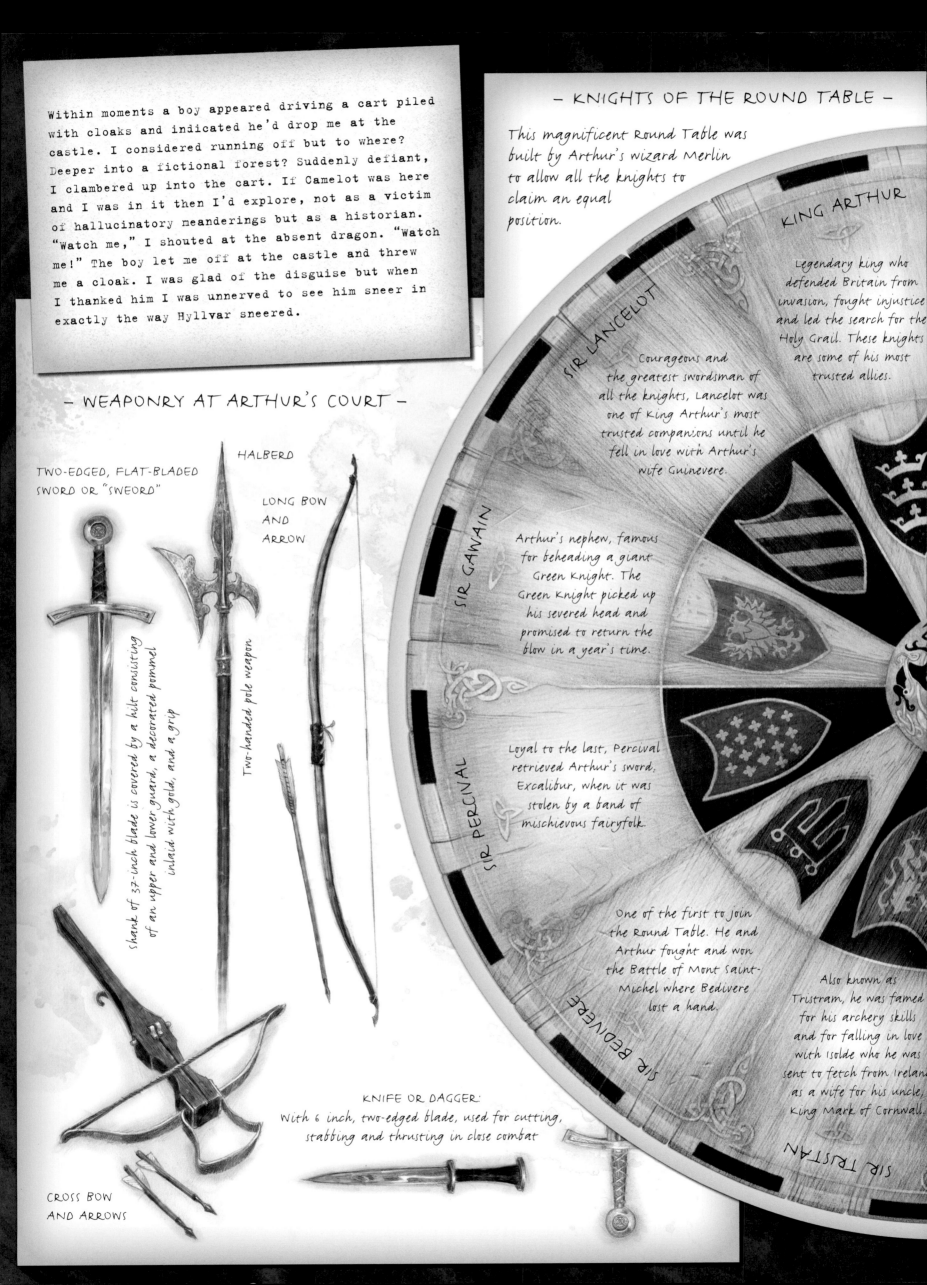

Within moments a boy appeared driving a cart piled with cloaks and indicated he'd drop me at the castle. I considered running off but to where? Deeper into a fictional forest? Suddenly defiant, I clambered up into the cart. If Camelot was here and I was in it then I'd explore, not as a victim of hallucinatory meanderings but as a historian. "Watch me," I shouted at the absent dragon. "Watch me!" The boy let me off at the castle and threw me a cloak. I was glad of the disguise but when I thanked him I was unnerved to see him sneer in exactly the way Hyllvar sneered.

– WEAPONRY AT ARTHUR'S COURT –

TWO-EDGED, FLAT-BLADED SWORD OR "SWEORD"

HALBERD

LONG BOW AND ARROW

Shank of 37-inch blade is covered by a hilt consisting of an upper and lower guard, a decorated pommel inlaid with gold, and a grip

Two-handed pole weapon

CROSS BOW AND ARROWS

KNIFE OR DAGGER:
With 6 inch, two-edged blade, used for cutting, stabbing and thrusting in close combat

– KNIGHTS OF THE ROUND TABLE –

This magnificent Round Table was built by Arthur's wizard Merlin to allow all the knights to claim an equal position.

KING ARTHUR

Legendary king who defended Britain from invasion, fought injustice and led the search for the Holy Grail. These knights are some of his most trusted allies.

SIR LANCELOT

Courageous and the greatest swordsman of all the knights, Lancelot was one of King Arthur's most trusted companions until he fell in love with Arthur's wife Guinevere.

SIR GAWAIN

Arthur's nephew, famous for beheading a giant Green Knight. The Green Knight picked up his severed head and promised to return the blow in a year's time.

SIR PERCIVAL

Loyal to the last, Percival retrieved Arthur's sword, Excalibur, when it was stolen by a band of mischievous fairyfolk.

SIR BEDIVERE

One of the first to join the Round Table. He and Arthur fought and won the Battle of Mont Saint-Michel where Bedivere lost a hand.

SIR TRISTAN

Also known as Tristram, he was famed for his archery skills and for falling in love with Isolde who he was sent to fetch from Ireland as a wife for his uncle, King Mark of Cornwall.

– A KNIGHT IN FULL ARMOUR –

PAULDRON: A shoulder guard. Mounted on leather and riveted for movement.

BARBUTE: Visorless war helmet with T-shaped opening for eyes and mouth

GAUNTLET: Attached to glove with rivets

BESAGEW: Armpit guard

GORGET: Neck guard

BREASTPLATE

SHIELD

COUTER: Elbow guard

HAUBERK: Protective shirt made from metal rings linked together

GREAVE: shin guard

LEATHER SCABBARD

SABATON: Foot guard

ROWEL SPUR

SIR GALAHAD

Arthur's most skilled swordsman who helped plan the quest for the Holy Grail.

SIR KAY

Known as Sir Kay the Tall, he was Arthur's foster brother and one of the first knights of the Round Table.

SIR PALAMEDES

Son of King Esclabor of Babylon, he was a hunter of the Questing Beast, the abominable monster that only the chosen could kill.

SIR LAMORAK

Son of King Pellinore and known for his strength and fiery temper. He single-handedly fought off more than 30 knights on several occasions.

SIR BORS

Cousin of Sir Lancelot, with a distinctive scar on his forehead. He proved himself worthy in the Quest for the Holy Grail.

SIR GERAINT

A prince of Devon who defeated the Knight of the Sparrow Hawk despite having only rusty, borrowed armour and sword.

SIDE WING

I spent hours studying the arms, armoury and the Round Table in the castle, until a great commotion erupted outside. Horses' hooves and yelping hounds brought stewards and knights running and I was carried out in the rush. Seeing swords drawn, I took to my heels and ran until the hard ground gave way to boggy marshland where I began to sink into a thick, brackish darkness. When at last I came up for air, I was sitting beside the log pile in the driveway, the dawn breaking. I was home but there was no trace of mud anywhere on my clothes or shoes. The Book, I decided, was the root cause of my troubles and had to be buried. I dashed inside, stuffed it into a bag, grabbed a spade, drove to the woods and started digging.

The Fourth World

Although exhausted on my return, instead of sleeping or celebrating I found myself scribbling notes about what I'd seen in Camelot. Then, as evening fell, I heard someone in the house. Peering into the living room, I was sure I saw my brother holding the Book and talking to himself. I burst in to confront him only to find it was Hyllvar. Narrowing his rheumy eyes, he held out the Book, which had not a speck of earth anywhere on it and said, "You would bury magic yet walk forever with the mundane?" The pages were open on a dire-looking place called the Dimskye Mountains. I began to protest but, looming close, Hyllvar steamed, "Home to me and my kind so you can hardly refuse. But take heart, tonight you will be at the controls." Clever, mind-reading Hyllvar. I liked nothing more than to be in the driver's seat and the fantasy firedrake knew it.

1

1. **Deep forest**
Hatchery and nursery hidden within

2. **Cave dormitories**
Accommodation for visiting beasts

3. **Abbey entrance**
A door no human could breach

THE DIMSKYE MOUNTAINS AND WYVERN ABBEY

Wyvern Abbey and the Dimskye Mountains provide a safe haven for the last of the living mythological beasts. Dragons from all over the world roam here along with chimeras, gryphons, hydras, cockatrices and basilisks. Deep in the forests the young are hatched, their instincts nurtured and survival skills taught. Cave dormitories for visiting creatures are built into the mountains. Those with wings challenge each other on extreme flying courses above the mountain peaks and precipices, while thunderbirds create local storms to test their endurance skills even further.

4. Highest mountains
For extreme flying challenges

5. Thunderbirds
The source of violent localised storms

6. Lookout point
Where beasts perch to watch for intruders

The Machine did most of the work flying to this wilderness inhabited by all the weird beasts that myth and legend have ever thrown at us. As we flew around it, Hyllvar pointed out characteristics of the various creatures like a tour guide. I was praying I'd not be asked to land the Machine but soon enough Hyllvar instructed me to bring us down near a dense wood. Here grotesque-looking cockerels were sitting on serpents' eggs, incubating basilisk babies. We watched as within minutes they hatched and although newly born were able to kill plants with their breath and cause birds to burst into flame with their gaze. They repulsed me but Hyllvar seemed to find them delightful. He even went over to some of the grown basilisks and had some kind of high-spirited exchange.

– HYDRA –
Origin: Lake of Lerna, Greece

Chop off one head and two grow in its place

Has many snake-like heads

Poisonous breath

Scent of its blood can kill

Scaly, serpent-like water monster

Grows to approx 35 feet

Goat head can grow from middle of body

Body of a lion

Snake-headed tail

Fire-breathing hybrid

Extremely strong

– CHIMERA –
Origin: Asia Minor

Grows to approx 8 feet in length

– CHINESE DRAGON –
Origin: East Asia

Deer-like antlers

Has auspicious powers and control over rainfall, typhoons and floods

Snake-like with four legs

Four claws to each foot

Capable of flight

Can grow to 40 feet in length

– RYŪ –
Origin: Japan

Huge, wingless water deity

Serpentine body covered in scales that are regularly shed

Long whiskers act as antennae or feelers

Three claws to each foot

Capable of flight

Grows to approx 30 feet in length

– BASILISK –
Origin: Europe

Poisonous breath

Cockerel's head with leathery comb

Can kill with a single glare

Wings of a dragon

Vulnerable to the odour of a weasel

Does not slither but runs on bird-like legs

Wingspan of approx 8 feet

– UNICORN –
Origin: Indus Valley

Horn has healing powers and purifies poisoned water

Long single horn between ears

Body of a white horse

Horn can grow to 28 inches long

– HIPPOGRIFF –
Origin: Greece

Half eagle half horse

Born of a mare and a gryphon

Extremely fast and capable fliers – able to reach the moon

– GRYPHON –
Origin: Egypt

Combination of lion and eagle gives it immense power

Famed as fearsome guardians

Eagle head and wings

Eagle talons on front legs

Body, tail and back legs of a lion

Wing span of approx 9 feet

Nests contain gold nuggets

Next Hyllvar directed me to fly us to the highest mountains to watch winged beasts challenge each other. Here the wind grew so fierce that I had to beg Hyllvar to take over and get us home. He refused. "I must stay. I have much to do. The Machine is yours. It will take you where you want to go." With that his presence beside me dissolved and in a flash of lightning I saw him materialise outside the craft, spread his great dragon wings and fly towards the Abbey. I was alone in the Machine but this was no time to feel abandoned. I had to survive and something came to me – an ancient Greek world I'd loved as a girl. I shouted at the control panel, "Atlantis! Take me to Atlantis!" It worked. The Machine shot like a bullet through the storm clouds into a clear blue sky and flew steadily like any normal aircraft through an entire day.

The Fifth World

The long journey gave me time to compose myself and consider. Each of these ventures was getting more precarious than the last and if the Book wouldn't stay buried then I had to find a way to get rid of Hyllvar. As if to arrest such a treacherous thought, the Machine clicked, pulsed and changed form. We hit black water and I was in a streamlined submersible descending to the ocean bed. Sheer amazement took over as the powerful lights penetrated the marine snow and floodlit the murky depths. Everywhere around me were the ruins of Atlantis and, in the distance, beyond fallen pillars, I saw what appeared to be Captain Nemo's submarine, the Nautilus. I could scarcely believe my eyes.

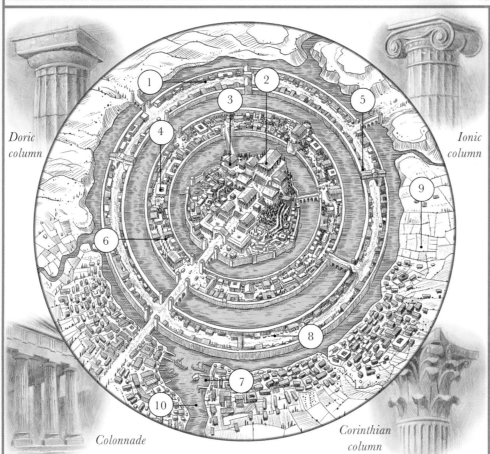

Doric column

Ionic column

Colonnade

Corinthian column

– THE CITY BEFORE IT SANK –

1. **Circles of land**
   Alternating concentric rings of land and water

2. **Temple to Poseidon**
   God of the Sea and father of King Atlas

3. **Palace of King Atlas**
   Ornately decorated

4. **Gymnasium**

5. **Army barracks**

6. **Public gardens**
   Fertile soil produces magnificent trees

7. **Harbour**

8. **Horse-racing course**
   Extends around entire island

9. **Agricultural fields**
   Irrigation system supports agriculture

10. **Canal to sea**

King Atlas, first ruler of Atlantis

ATLANTIS AND THE NAUTILUS

According to Plato, the ancient Greek philosopher, Atlantis was an island in the Atlantic Ocean where people lived in an age of harmony and abundance. In time they became greedy and schemed to conquer lands to every side, including the mighty state of Athens. This so angered Zeus, king of the Greek gods, that he ordered up an earthquake of such magnitude that it sank the entire island within twenty-four hours.

Giant octopuses, jellyfish, sharks and spider crabs swim around columns built of red, white and black rock originally covered in precious metals. Now, the only light amongst the fallen gates, temples and bridges is the glow from bioluminescent deep-sea creatures. At times light shines out from the portholes of Captain Nemo's submarine, the Nautilus, as he explores marine life around the sunken city.

As if it sensed my interest, the submersible took me over to the Nautilus which I knew well from a diagram my brother had on his bedroom wall as a child. We moved from porthole to porthole before entering and locking into the docking bay. I could hardly breathe with anticipation as the hatch opened and I was able to step straight down into the Nautilus itself. With every detail of its layout in my head I found my way past the room where sea water is distilled, past the laboratory and up to the Captain's Quarters where Captain Nemo stores his marine specimens.

– DRAGONFISH –

Dragonfish start life on the surface of the ocean. They descend to the depths after they grow capable of producing their own bioluminescent light.

THE NAUTILUS

BUILT BY CAPTAIN NEMO IN PURSUIT OF FREEDOM AND KNOWLEDGE

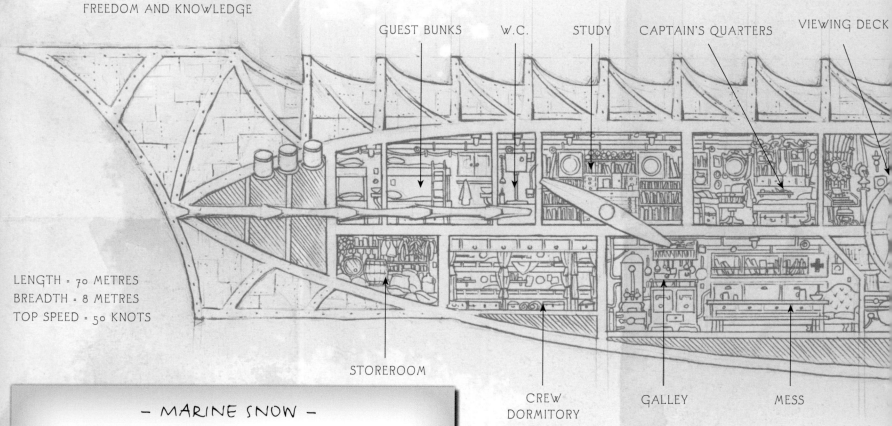

GUEST BUNKS W.C. STUDY CAPTAIN'S QUARTERS VIEWING DECK

LENGTH = 70 METRES
BREADTH = 8 METRES
TOP SPEED = 50 KNOTS

STOREROOM

CREW DORMITORY GALLEY MESS

– MARINE SNOW –

A continuous shower of mainly biological detritus that falls to the aphotic (lightless) zones from the light-rich photic zones higher up. It is an important food source for deep-sea creatures. The Nautilus, namesake of Nemo's sub, lives here.

– SUBMARINE BUOYANCY –

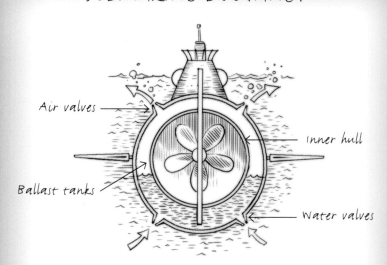

Air valves

Inner hull

Ballast tanks

Water valves

A submarine can vary the quantity of air and water in its ballast tanks in order to float or dive. More air makes the submarine surface, less means it will dive.

– ATOLLA JELLYFISH –

Nicknamed the alarm jellyfish as when threatened by a predator, the Atolla emits a flashing blue light that attracts larger predators to attack the threat to the Atolla.

– GIANT BIOLUMINESCENT SQUID –

Photophores or light organs are found all over the squid's body, including its eyes, internal organs, funnel and tentacles.

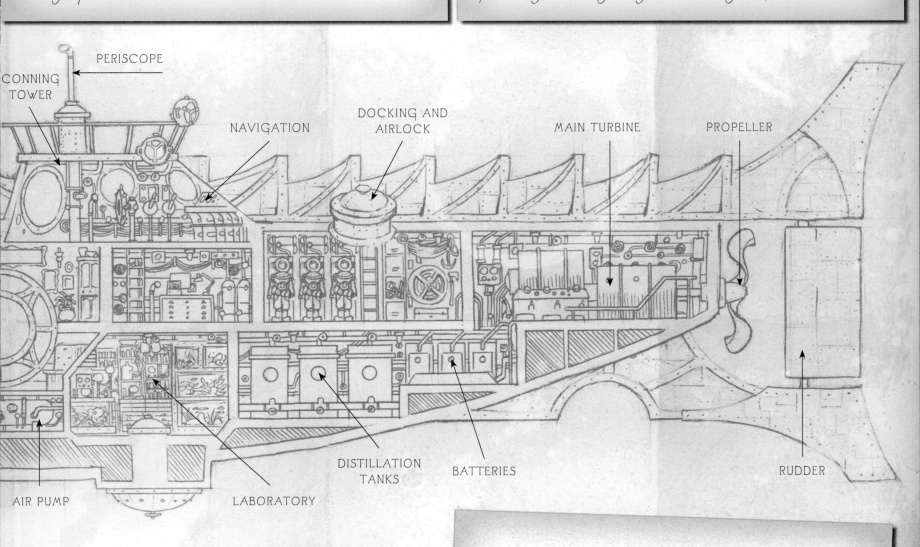

PERISCOPE

CONNING TOWER

NAVIGATION

DOCKING AND AIRLOCK

MAIN TURBINE

PROPELLER

DISTILLATION TANKS

BATTERIES

RUDDER

AIR PUMP

LABORATORY

– DISTILLATION TANKS –

Turn salty sea water into pure drinking water.

I was so aghast I could not resist gathering some specimens to take home. In my excitement, I dropped one of the jars and it smashed. Footsteps approached and I heard urgent voices. I had to move fast and, dropping the rest, I darted behind a grandfather clock. As crew members burst in, I slipped out through the open door and ran. Reaching my submersible, I put my head on the control panel and whispered urgently, "Get me out of here." Nothing happened. The crew's voices got louder and closer. I was going to be discovered and meet my end on the ocean floor centuries before I'd ever been alive. I begged again, swearing to believe in magic, dragons and imaginary lands if it would only move. This time it dislodged, rapidly rose to the surface, transformed and took me home.

The Sixth World

I went to bed in much confusion, my head exploding. I'd visited five imaginary worlds and they'd been as real as my hand in front of me. In this battle between what could and couldn't be, the scientist appeared to be losing. Normally, anything irrational is anathema to me, and yet that evening when the Book opened on Lilliput and the Machine flashed its lights in the driveway, I put up no opposition. It seemed these nine nights would take their course whatever I did and so I let myself be flown into bright skies over sparkling seas. The craft turned into something resembling a magnificent hot air balloon and I was suspended there looking down with genuine curiosity on an island of miniature people.

Penny

Comb

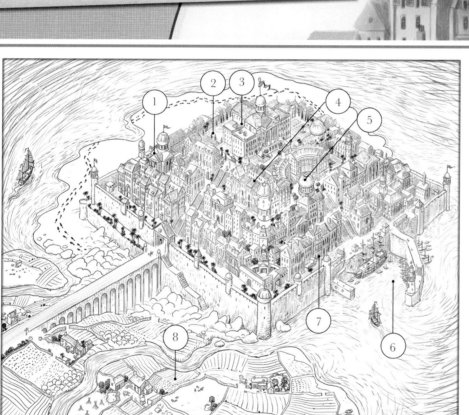

– MILDENDO, CAPITAL CITY OF LILLIPUT –

1. **Palace of the Emperor of Lilliput**
   Home to the mighty Golbasto Momarem Evlame Gurdilo Shefin Mully Ully Gue

2. **Golbasto Square**
   Main town square. Markets and festivals held here.

3. **Parliament building**
   Where the two opposing parties sit – the High-Heels and the Low-Heels

4. **Momarem Avenue**
   Home to the government offices

5. **Rope-dancing arena**
   Where the Emperor selects his government ministers

6. **Naval headquarters & harbour**
   Under the command of Admiral Skyresh Bolgolam

7. **Seafront parade**
   With outdoor attractions and amusements

8. **Farmlands**
   Supplying freshly grown produce for the town

Handkerchief

Buttons

Pencil

LILLIPUT – A MINIATURE WORLD

Lilliput is an island kingdom where everything is as tiny as the people, none of whom are taller than 6 inches. Despite their miniature stature they are as self-important, corrupt, envious, greedy and ridiculous as many full-sized men and women. In this, their essentially mad Emperor leads the way. Lilliputians are reputed to be talented engineers who build their own war machines, although these are so small they are only of use against other tiny people. Many years ago a full-sized surgeon named Lemuel Gulliver washed up on the shore and to this day some of his possessions, left behind or stolen from him, are treated as amusements, curiosities and artefacts of historic interest.

The balloon began to drift and lurch dangerously and I took control. Though a machine from some far-flung future, it worked on the principle of thermodynamics like any hot air balloon - which luckily I understood. To keep airborne I had to open the valve in the burner and let the propane gas flow, fire the flames and release hot air into the balloon envelope. By pulling the chord attached to the flap at the top of the balloon I could let the heated air gradually escape and slowly descend. This way I came down as low as I dared and got an unexpected view of a doll's house world where at least three adults could sleep in one of my shoes and fifty of their chickens would probably fit into one of my pockets.

– SUITABILITY TO SERVE –

The Emperor judges the suitability of applicants for government office by their ability to dance on a rope 12 inches above the ground.

– LAWS OF LILLIPUT, NO 6 –
Cracking eggs

This law was passed after the Emperor's grandfather cut his finger on the shell while cracking a boiled egg on its big end. Now all eggs must be cracked on the small end. Those who disobey are called Big-Endians (in contrast to Small-Endians) and risk arrest if caught.

– PARLIAMENTARY PARTIES –
High-Heels and Low-Heels

The two political parties are recognised by the heels on their shoes. Supporters of the Emperor wear low heels and the opposition wear high heels. The Emperor's son wears one high and one low heel so no one can tell which side he is on.

– SIZE AND SCALE COMPARISONS –

IN OUR WORLD

IN LILLIPUT

Pea pod and peas

Cannon and cannon balls

House fly

Lilliputian bird

A puppy

Lilliputian elephant

– UPSIDE DOWN BURIALS –

Lilliputians believe the world is flat and will eventually flip over. When this happens, they believe their dead will come back to life, so they bury them head down. This means when the Flip occurs the dead will already be standing on their feet.

– CORNER TO CORNER WRITING –

Unlike anyone else in the known world, Lilliputians write aslant, from one corner of the page to the other.

My urge to laugh at these tiny, none-too-bright people who happily obeyed ridiculous laws soon ended. I accidentally let out too much hot air and descended too low over the town. At the sight of an airborne giantess the entire town came out armed with bows and arrows which they fired at the Machine in great volleys. As I marvelled at the tiny projectiles dropping all around me, the balloon began to collapse for it had been punctured in so many places. I felt us fall, plunging into the ocean, and this time I was not returned to safety as dawn broke. I was bobbing about in the sea in a cracked craft that was rapidly taking in water.

The seventh World

The sun was dipping, the water icy. The Machine had failed as I feared it would in Atlantis and I only had myself to blame. I'd weakened, given in to the impossible and now, soaked to the skin and sinking fast, my whole life flashed in front of me. It was all over. I was going to drown, meet a watery grave - or would I only imagine it? I had no idea but if I did drown at least it would teach my interfering brother a lesson. In that moment, a flock of gulls appeared above me and above them the strangest sight yet - a flying island. This was undoubtedly Laputa, which Gulliver had also visited. I saw fishermen sitting on the island's edge, long lines from their fishing rods dropping into the sea. If I could just get their attention, I might yet be saved.

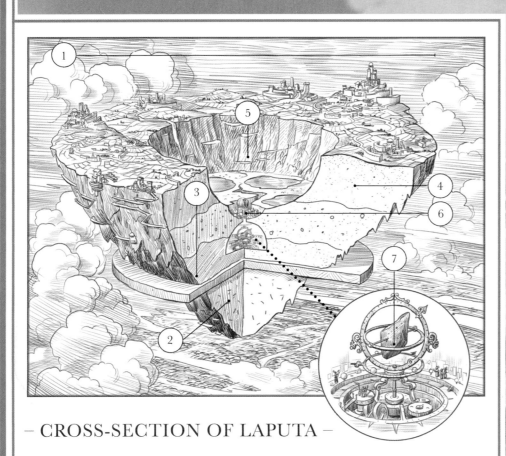

– CROSS-SECTION OF LAPUTA –

1. **Diameter of 4.5 miles**

2. **Layer of adamantine rock**
   200 yards thick

3. **Layers of minerals and rock**
   Galena (PbS)
   Pyrite (FeS₂)
   Chalcopyrite (CuFeS₂)
   Bauxite
   Magnetite (Fe₃O₄)

4. **Rich earth**
   10-12 feet deep

5. **Slope from circumference to centre**
   Allows rain to run down into four large water basins

6. **Astronomical observatory**
   Situated 100 yards underground

7. **Magnetic lodestone**
   Enabling the movement of the island

THE FLYING ISLAND OF LAPUTA

Laputa is an island kingdom that flies. Its movements are controlled by astronomers using a huge lodestone poised on an axle of adamantine rock so angled that even the weakest hand can turn it. The lodestone contains a powerful magnet that works with the earth's magnetic poles to keep it moving. The island is ruled by a tyrannical king with little to no common sense and inhabited by people who worship music, mathematics and astronomy, decorate everything they wear with images of celestial bodies, and fashion every item of food into a geometric shape or musical instrument. However, having the concentration span of a colony of gnats, the Laputians are never able to apply their interests to any useful purpose.

I shouted and waved until the fishermen noticed and let down a rope ladder. Once I'd struggled out of the sinking balloon machine, I scaled the ladder with uncharacteristic speed lest they change their minds. They showed no hostility when I arrived and quickly ushered me into the town and the house of a well-to-do citizen who gave me dry clothes and plied me with items of bizarrely shaped food. Afterwards he gave me a tour where I witnessed the Laputians' obsession with music, mathematics and astronomy and saw the remarkable workings of a magnetised lodestone – the very engine of the island.

– MAGNETIC LODESTONE –

Lodestone – 6 yards long

Attracting end set at oblique angle – the island moves on a parallel line to the angle

Axle

Mechanism for turning the lodestone

When the attracting end of the lodestone is pointing downwards, the island descends; when pointing upwards, the island rises.

– MEASURING INSTRUMENTS –

ASTROLABE: for making astronomical measurements of the altitudes of celestial bodies

ORRERY: clockwork model of the solar system

COMPASS: instrument with pointer showing direction of magnetic north

OCTANT: navigation instrument that measures altitude of celestial bodies, using mirrors to double the angle that can be observed

BACKSTAFF: keeping the sun to their backs, users can measure altitude of the sun and moon by observing the shadows cast by the shadow vane on the horizon vane

shadow vane

Horizon vane

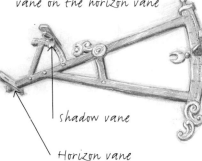

SEXTANT: navigation and survey instrument measuring the angular distance between celestial bodies and the horizon

– EXAMPLES OF LAPUTAN FOOD –

Geometric-shaped breads

Oboe-shaped sausages

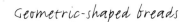

Harp-shaped vegetable pie

Mutton triangle

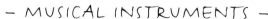

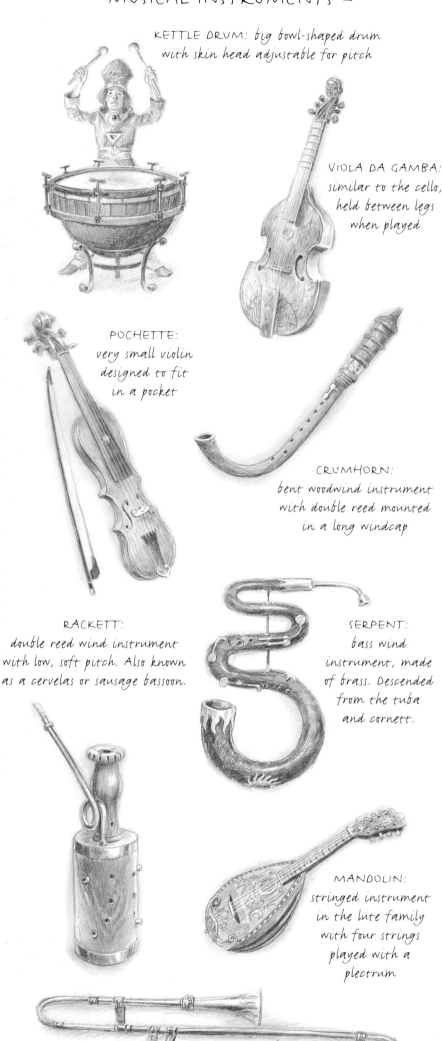

KETTLE DRUM: big bowl-shaped drum with skin head adjustable for pitch

VIOLA DA GAMBA: similar to the cello, held between legs when played

POCHETTE: very small violin designed to fit in a pocket

CRUMHORN: bent woodwind instrument with double reed mounted in a long windcap

RACKETT: double reed wind instrument with low, soft pitch. Also known as a cervelas or sausage bassoon.

SERPENT: bass wind instrument, made of brass. Descended from the tuba and cornett.

MANDOLIN: stringed instrument in the lute family with four strings played with a plectrum

SACKBUT: related to the trombone, with a telescopic slide to vary the length of the tube and change pitch

– GEOMETRIC SHAPES –

POLYGONS (two-dimensional): triangle (fig. 1), pentagon (fig. 2)

Fig. 1   Fig. 2

POLYHEDRONS (three-dimensional): cube (fig. 3), pyramid (fig. 4), tetrahedron (fig. 5)

Fig. 3   Fig. 4   Fig. 5

ELLIPSOIDS (three-dimensional bound by curved surfaces): spheroid (fig. 6), sphere (fig. 7)

Fig. 6   Fig. 7

QUADRILATERALS (all with 4 sides, 4 vertices and angles that total 360°): kite (fig. 8), trapezium (fig. 9), rhombus (fig. 10),

Fig. 9   Fig. 10   Fig. 8

TROCHOIDS AND CURVES: epicycloid (fig. 11), cycloid (fig. 12), brachistochrone (fig. 13), roulette (fig. 14)

Fig. 11   Fig. 12   Fig. 13   Fig. 14

When I'd marvelled sufficiently, he took me to see the King who was greatly confused by my presence. First, he presented me with an oboe-shaped sausage and a small brass astrolabe as if I were an honoured guest but when I thanked him he grew furious and yelled for the guards. Imagining a damp dungeon with nothing but rats and cockroaches for company I ran, jumped the palace balcony and dropped, landing in the boughs of a tall oak tree. Swaying there precariously I found I had not been deserted after all. The balloon machine, miraculously restored, drifted into sight with Hyllvar standing serenely in the bubble dome. He brought it over to the tree so I could clamber in. And I have to admit I'd never been so glad to see anyone ... condescending and impossible as that dragon was.

The Eighth World

As if he sensed I'd softened, the next night Hyllvar had the audacity to be sitting, at ease, in my favourite armchair. As I entered he steamed, "Imagination is the only guide to discovery and a great companion to anyone stuck in a rut." His tone was so complacent, I snapped, "I've nearly died on these travels of yours. Why should I listen to anything you say?" "But you didn't die," Hyllvar sighed. "One day you will but for now do not leave yourself unchanged. Finish what has started or return to your old life mired in loneliness and denial." He opened the Book and showed me a vista of an island called Buyan and soon enough we were on our way to it, flying over calm seas. The Machine turned into a small longboat as a giant whale rose from the waves and behind that came mountains and forests, spires, towers, domes and cupolas until the whole island was visible.

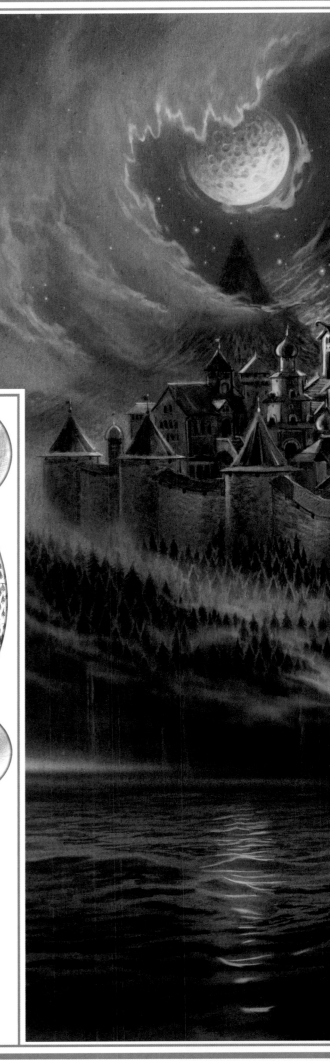

The Sun

Prince Gvidon

The Three Winds

The Swan Princess

– THE MAP –

1. **Walled city of Ledenets**
   Filled with domed buildings in the Russian style

2. **The sacred oak tree**
   Hiding place of the soul of Koschei the Deathless

3. **The Alatyr**
   A sacred white stone with magical powers marking the centre of the universe

4. **Healing rivers**
   Flowing from under the Alatyr

5. **Weather source**
   All the world's weather is created here by the god Perun

6. **Enchanted forests**
   Where mythical creatures roam free

BUYAN, THE FIRST ISLAND

According to Slavic tradition, Buyan is the first island to have emerged from the primeval ocean. Using the tides and the North, West and East Winds that originated here, the island can disappear if threatened and reappear when the threat has passed. The buildings with their double domes and graceful cupolas line the steep winding streets of Ledenets, a walled city surrounded by enchanted forests filled with many fabulous creatures. The island is also home to the Alatyr, a stone with magical powers. Legend has it that the city was created for Prince Gvidon Saltanovich by a beautiful Swan Princess whom he'd rescued from the claws of a bird of prey.

In a low voice, Hyllvar activated two sets of silver oars and, strangely companionable, we rowed together to a fine white beach and went ashore. The beauty, the peace, the mystery of the place worked a strange alchemy. I felt myself melt into the surroundings, becoming the water, the grass, the bird song. This ethereal, out-of-body state was shattered by the sound of thundering hooves crashing through the undergrowth. I froze and a thorn thicket sprang up around me as if at the bidding of one of Buyan's magical beings.

– GODDESS OF THE MORNING STAR –

Zorya Utrennyaya, Goddess of the Morning Star, can be seen paddling in a golden canoe early every morning. She serves the Sun God, Dazbog, and opens the gates of the palace at dawn to let out the sun-chariot.

– INDRIK, PROTECTOR OF ANIMALS –

With the body of a bull and the head of a horse, Indrik is the protector of all animals and can dispose of enemies and help heroes find treasure.

– GODDESS OF THE EVENING STAR –

Zorya Vechernyaya, Goddess of the Evening Star, closes the sun God's palace gates each evening after his chariot returns. she and Utrennyaya guard the doomsday hound, Simargl, ensuring he does not break his chains and bring the world to an end.

– THE ALATYR –

A sacred white stone, guarded by the bird Gagana with her iron beak and copper claws and the serpent Garafina who has the antidote to all snake bites. Two rivers flow from beneath the Alatyr with powers to heal diseases. Their beds are lined with white pebbles that shine from within.

– GAMAYUN –

Gamayun is a bird with a woman's face who knows everything about everyone. She has prophetic powers and carries messages from the gods across the world.

– KOSCHEI THE DEATHLESS –

Koschei is an old, wiry, wild man who steals the souls of others while remaining immortal himself. To protect himself from death, his soul is hidden on the point of a needle inside an egg which is inside a duck which is inside a hare which is inside a chest buried under the sacred oak tree of Buyan. If the chest is dug up and opened the hare will run away, and if the hare is caught and killed the duck will fly off.

From there I watched as a half-horse half-bull came tearing through the trees carrying a wild-looking man whom I realised later must be Koschei, the soul stealer. Brandishing a heavy sword he slashed at the thicket meant to protect me. I felt I was in a hundred pieces which in that instant I knew would never be reassembled as they once were. Dazed and bewildered, a stranger to myself, I somehow made my way back to the boat where Hyllvar took the oars and rowed us away. Under the warm sun, with him in control, I grew calm until in a burst of confused emotions I realised that if Buyan was the eighth of these fantastical journeys, there was only one more journey left and one more world to see.

The Ninth World

We travelled through an entire day until, as evening fell, the silence was shattered by a mighty uproar. The sky filled with an army of winged horses ridden by women in armour, their red cloaks flying like bloodied clouds behind them. "The Valkyries," said Hyllvar, "carrying the souls of fallen heroes to Valhalla, Hall of the Slain, in Asgard." "Can we see it?" I called. "I fear not," Hyllvar barked. "The Machine only had the power to reach eight worlds. This is the ninth. I misjudged it." I was stunned. "But how will I get home?" I cried as Hyllvar began to fade in front of my eyes. "Hyllvar! Stay with me!" I yelled, my mind churning. "I know! I could climb onto your back! You could fly us to Valhalla and then on home!" I swear I heard him chuckle as he steamed, "You have addressed me by my name at last. But are you sure you want to fly on the back of a fantasy firedrake?" I was sure. Surer of that than of anything ever.

Valkyries carrying the spirits of the fallen

1. **Valhalla** – *The immense hall with 540 doors, a ceiling lined with shields and glistening spears for rafters*

2. **Bifrost** – *Guarded by Heimdall, the gods' watchman, the rainbow bridge connects Asgard with Midgard, the realm of humans*

VALHALLA, IN ASGARD

Valhalla, Hall of the Slain, is in Asgard, the highest of the nine realms in Yggdrasil, the great tree of life in Norse mythology. Asgard is ruled by the god Odin and his wife, the goddess Frigg. It is lush with shady forests and exotic plant life. Jewels and precious stones line every pathway. At the centre lies the Plain of Splendour called Idavoll, where the gods have built Valhalla along with temples, palaces and metal works to forge every kind of tong and tool.

Directed by Odin, the Valkyries choose who will live or die in combat and then bring back the spirits of the chosen ones to live at Valhalla until the final battle during Ragnarok, the Doom of the Gods and End of the World.

3. Glasir – *The most beautiful of all trees, bearing red and gold leaves*

4. Yggdrasil – *These are the highest branches of the Tree of Life*

5. Idavoll – *The plain where the gods have built shrines and temples*

I kicked off my shoes and clambered onto Hyllvar's back. At once I was ten years old again, filled with wonder, fear and excitement as we soared after the Valkyries to the Hall of Valhalla. We landed on the roof without attracting attention. From behind Hyllvar's horns I saw the Valkyries dismount, remove their saddlebags containing the spirits of their fallen heroes and carry them into Valhalla to live for ever. The idea of the fallen being lifted up and carried to safety must have triggered what happened next. In vivid detail, I saw what I had blocked out years ago.

– ODIN AND FRIGG –

ODIN, highest of the Aesir gods, ruler of all and personifying air, wisdom and victory

FRIGG, meaning "Beloved". Odin's wife, goddess of love, marriage and destiny

– YGGDRASIL –
The nine realms of the Norse world tree

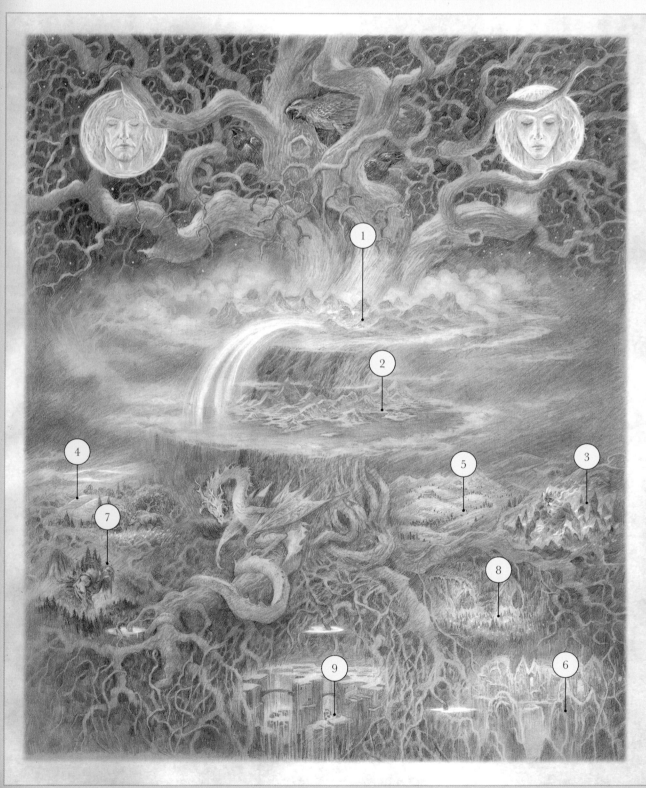

1. **ASGARD**
   The highest realm, home to the Aesir tribe of gods and goddesses and ruled by the god Odin and his wife the goddess Frigg

2. **ALFHEIM**
   Home to light elves and ruled by Lord Freyr, god of fertility and peace

3. **MUSPELHEIM**
   A realm of terrible heat and flames, home to the fire giants and ruled by the giant Surt

4. **VANAHEIM**
   Home of the Vanir gods, masters of magic, nature and foretelling the future. Sworn enemies of the Aesir.

5. **MIDGARD**
   Home to humans and connected to Asgard by Bifrost, the rainbow bridge

6. **NIFLHEIM**
   A world of mist, fog, darkness and cold

7. **JOTUNHEIM**
   Home of the giants ruled by Thrym and separated from Asgard by a river that never freezes

8. **SVARTALFHEIM**
   Home of the dwarfs, master smiths who live in underground caves

9. **HELHEIM**
   A cold realm ruled by the goddess Hel, where many dead are sent

shields line the ceiling between
rafters of glistening spears

The dead who reside here –
the einherjar – live like
Viking warriors, fighting
each other all day only to
find their wounds healed
each evening

The entrance is guarded
by fierce wolves and
Glasir, the tree of gold

Great feasts are held nightly with meat
from Saehrimnir, the wild boar, who
comes back to life each morning to be
butchered again for the next evening

seats made of
breastplates surround
the dining tables

Elaborately carved pillars support
the gold-bright vaulted roof

I saw myself, as a girl, with my little brother Tom, on the big
dipper at the funfair. He was terrified but I was with friends and
threatened him with horrible things if he didn't come with us. He was
crying while we giggled in delight when suddenly there was a great
screeching and lurching and the train came away from its rails. Our
carriage was thrown into the air and, with all of us screaming, it
crashed through a hoarding to the ground below. I blamed myself for
the injuries Tom suffered through my selfish need to have the upper
hand. I withdrew, keeping away from everyone, dedicating myself to
the sciences which held no unexpected horrors. Cold reasoning and
hard facts became my universe. As if Hyllvar saw what I was seeing,
he steamed softly, "Let it go. You all survived." "But..." I started.
"But a million things," he said. "Anything can happen, any time. It
is certainty that is the desolate place. And once there, the only way
out is on the wings of imagination. Or, you could say, on the back of
me." I began to sob. He did not look round but said faintly, "Now we
see you are not dead inside. The demon is faced. Our work is done."

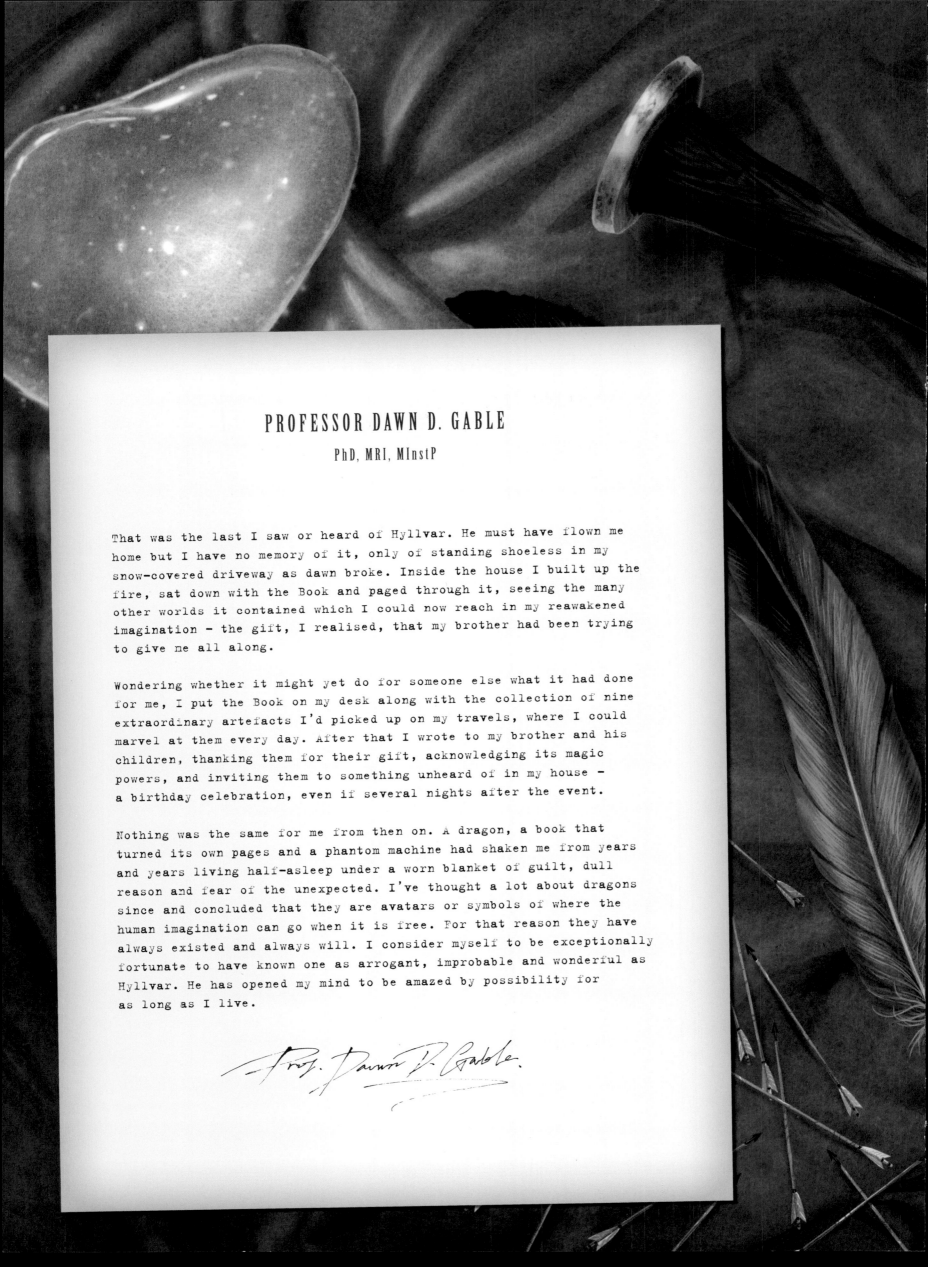

PROFESSOR DAWN D. GABLE

PhD, MRI, MInstP

That was the last I saw or heard of Hyllvar. He must have flown me home but I have no memory of it, only of standing shoeless in my snow-covered driveway as dawn broke. Inside the house I built up the fire, sat down with the Book and paged through it, seeing the many other worlds it contained which I could now reach in my reawakened imagination – the gift, I realised, that my brother had been trying to give me all along.

Wondering whether it might yet do for someone else what it had done for me, I put the Book on my desk along with the collection of nine extraordinary artefacts I'd picked up on my travels, where I could marvel at them every day. After that I wrote to my brother and his children, thanking them for their gift, acknowledging its magic powers, and inviting them to something unheard of in my house – a birthday celebration, even if several nights after the event.

Nothing was the same for me from then on. A dragon, a book that turned its own pages and a phantom machine had shaken me from years and years living half-asleep under a worn blanket of guilt, dull reason and fear of the unexpected. I've thought a lot about dragons since and concluded that they are avatars or symbols of where the human imagination can go when it is free. For that reason they have always existed and always will. I consider myself to be exceptionally fortunate to have known one as arrogant, improbable and wonderful as Hyllvar. He has opened my mind to be amazed by possibility for as long as I live.

Prof. Dawn D. Gable.

Hyllvar Imagination Prize awarded to debut novel by 18 year old

By D. N. Primmer, Culture Editor

YESTERDAY, the Hyllvar Prize for Imaginative Writing was won by 18-year-old Maria Knowles for her first novel, "Where Birds Go To Die". The prize was set up by Professor Dawn Gable to celebrate "the power of the imagination when it takes flight". The Professor, who died last year, was a theoretical physicist who achieved prominence relatively late in life for her innovative approach in the field of Space-Time Continuity. Writing under the pseudonym Hyllvar Hunt she also became a bestselling author, writing nine books set in nine fantasy worlds that won her legions of devoted readers across the world. When asked to comment, Maria Knowles said she had been inspired to let her imagination go wild after reading "Quarkrise", "Song of the Sawtooth Sisters" and "The Lawbreakers of Yo" by Hyllvar Hunt. Maria is already planning her next book and said that the award will enable her to "reach for the stars when it comes to writing". The prize is awarded annually and open to all ages, genders and nationalities. ∎